SCHOLASTIC Phonics

All Sorts of Nests

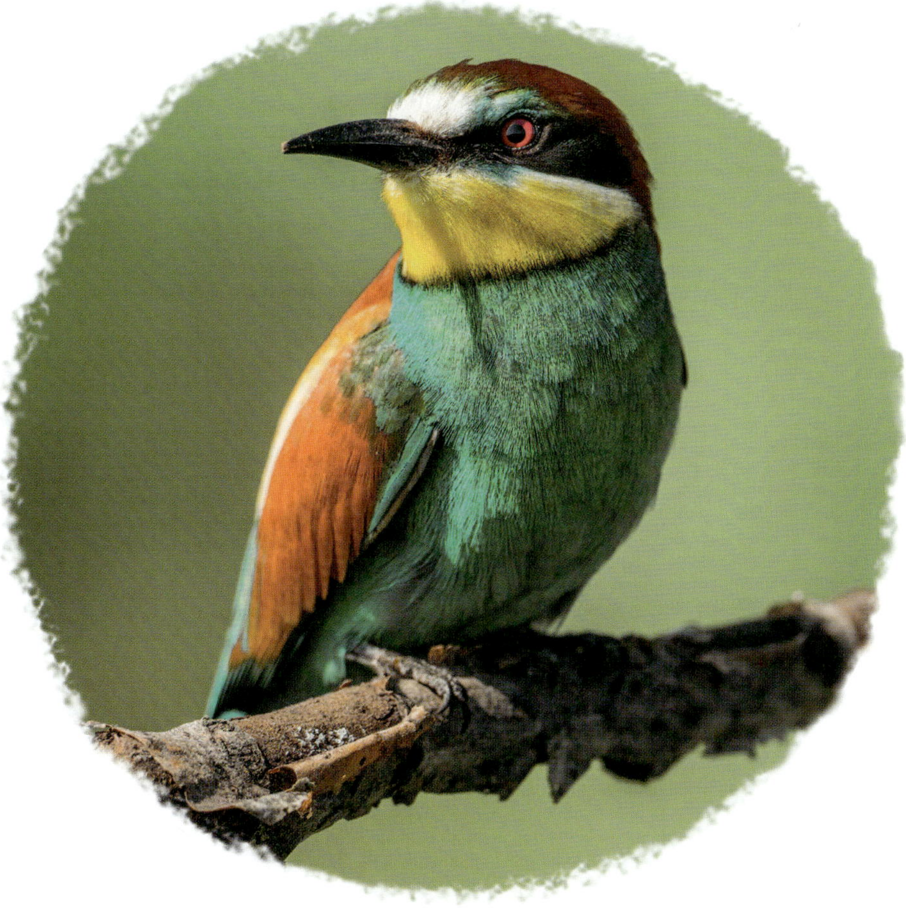

Published in the UK by Scholastic Education, 2023
Scholastic Distribution Centre, Bosworth Avenue, Tournament Fields, Warwick, CV34 6UQ
Scholastic Ireland, 89E Lagan Road, Dublin Industrial Estate, Glasnevin, Dublin, D11 HP5F

SCHOLASTIC and associated logos are trademarks and/or registered trademarks of Scholastic Inc.
www.scholastic.co.uk
© 2023 Scholastic
1 2 3 4 5 6 7 8 9   3 4 5 6 7 8 9 0 1 2

Printed by Ashford Colour Press
The book is made of materials from well-managed, FSC®-certified forests and other controlled sources.

A CIP catalogue record for this book is available from the British Library.
ISBN 978-0702-32101-6

All rights reserved. This book is sold subject to the condition that it shall not, by way of trade or otherwise, be lent, hired out or otherwise circulated in any form of binding or cover other than that in which it is published. No part of this publication may be reproduced, stored in a retrieval system, or transmitted in any form or by any other means (electronic, mechanical, photocopying, recording or otherwise) without prior written permission of Scholastic.

Every effort has been made to trace copyright holders for the works reproduced in this publication, and the publishers apologise for any inadvertent omissions.

Author
Rachel Russ

Editorial team
Rachel Morgan, Vicki Yates, Alison Gilbert, Jennie Clifford

Design team
Dipa Mistry, Andrea Lewis, We Are Grace

Photographs
Cover lavin photography/iStock
p4 (nest in tree) LIUDMYLA PISHCHIKOVA/Shutterstock
p4 (nest on electricity cable) Bob Hilscher/Shutterstock
p5 DE1967/iStock
p6 goran_safarek/Shutterstock
p8 (swiftlet) Tony Tilford/Shutterstock
p8 (nest) finchfocus/Shutterstock
p9 ThamKC/Shutterstock
p10–11 Richard Seeley/Shutterstock
p3, 12 Rich Carey/Shutterstock
p13 Rainer Lesniewski/Shutterstock
p14 (bee-eater on branch) Hekla/Shutterstock
p1, 14 (bee-eater in nest) Siarhei Zuyonak/Shutterstock
p15 Albert Beukhof/Shutterstock
p16–17, 24 balticboy/iStock
p18 (inset) Ondrej Prosicky/Shutterstock
p18–19, 24 Beate Wolter/Shutterstock
p20 Aquaterra/Shutterstock
p21 kojihirano/iStock
p22 (dunnock) Alan Tunnicliffe/Shutterstock
p22 (starling) LS92/Shutterstock
p23 Marcin Mierzejewski/Shutterstock

Help your child to read!

This book practises these letters and letter sounds.
Point and say the sounds with your child:

(ay (as in 'lays')) (ou (as in 'found')) (ea (as in 'beak')) (ir (as in 'bird'))

Your child may need help to read these common tricky words:

(all) (of) (the) (so) (be) (like) (you) (what) (are)
(by) (to) (some) (one)

Before reading
- Look at the cover picture and read the title together. Read the back cover blurb to your child.
- Ask your child: *What do you know about birds' nests? Where do birds make nests?*
- Talk about the image in the magnifying glass.

During reading
- If your child gets stuck on a word, remind them to sound it out and then blend the sounds to read the word: w-ea-v-er, weaver.
- If they are still stuck, show them how to read the word.
- Enjoy looking at the pictures together. Pause to talk about the information.

After reading
- Talk about the images on page 24. What can your child tell you about them?
- Ask your child: *Where do bee-eaters nest?*
- Discuss which nest your child found most interesting or surprising.

Birds construct all sorts of nests!

The long-tailed tit collects moss for its neat nest.

It coats the nest in green things so it will not be seen.

This stops bigger birds, like jays, eating its eggs.

Can you tell what the swiftlet forms its nest from? Spit!

Swiftlet nests are eaten by humans and this can be bad for the birds and the eggs.

The hummingbird's firm nest is constructed using twigs and cobwebs. At first, the eggs just fit.
As the chicks get bigger, cobwebs help the nest to expand.

This weaver bird connects leaf strips to a tree with its beak.
It needs lots of leaf strips for its nest.

Some weaver birds form one big nest. Three hundred birds can stay in it!

The bee-eater digs its nest in a sandbank.

This owl digs a nest too! It is underground.

From underground to up high…

...a stork's nest can be found on a rooftop!

This bird lays its eggs on a floating nest.

eggs

The woodpecker nests in a round gap in a tree trunk.

This woodpecker has formed its nest in an odd spot. It's in a cactus!

In spring, look for a bird with twigs in its beak.

It may be starting its nest!

Talk about it!